WHAT IS MAN

TUMISANG MABE

TUMISANG MABE

Since 2023

Paperback: ISBN: 9798230797623

Amazon ISBN: 9798203797623

Hardcover: ISBN: 9798870140728

Contents

Introduction
Chapter 1

Chapter 2

The Spirit of Man

Chapter 3

The Body of Man

Introduction

The human being is an extraordinary creature, often regarded as complex synthesis—"beyond" that which is physical. The creation of man is divided into three fundamental aspects: soul, spirit, and body, each playing a pivotal role in essence of human existence. The soul encompasses the mind, will and emotions, housing various faculties that contribute to the creation of man. Among these faculties we have:

• Imagination — plays a crucial role, enabling us to bring forth ideas into tangible realities or it is what we use to take an idea—something that is non-physical and turn it into something material.

• Perception — another essential faculty, dictates the manner in which we interpret things, uses both conscious and subconscious processes.

• Intuition — serves as an internal guide, often described as the subtle voice that imparts truth.

• Reasoning — facilitates critical thinking, analysis, and comparative evaluation of ideas and events.

• Memory — operates as the repository for past experiences, ideas, and information, allowing for learning and reflection.

Moreover, man is fundamentally a spirit, representing the core dimension of human identity. This spiritual aspect is interface through which men engage with God and the spiritual realm, using the inherent senses of faith, hope, and prayer. The spirit also possesses a subconscious mind.

Man possesses a physical body that interacts with the material world through the five senses of: sight, smell, hearing, taste, and touch. Scientific research indicates that our mental processes, emotions, and will are intricately linked to the body through our endocrine, nervous, and immune systems. Additionally, scripture emphasizes a significant relationship among our physical, emotional, and spiritual well-being. As noted in Proverbs 17:22, "A cheerful heart is good medicine, but a crushed spirit dries up bones."

Chapter 1

The Soul of Man

The soul is a spirit that is conscious because of the mind, and it is eternal. There is often confusion about the human spirit and the human soul. In places, scripture seems to use the terms interchangeably, but there has to be subtle difference. Otherwise how could the Word penetrate "even to dividing soul and spirit?" The body houses the spirit and the soul, which are the real parts of man. The soul is the connecter between the body and spirit. The soul has different faculties or attributes which are: Wisdom and understanding The soul has understanding, wisdom and knowledge, induction and reasoning. Wisdom is one of those qualities that are difficult to define, because it encompasses so much, but people generally recognize it when they come to its atmosphere. It is encountered mostly in the realm of decision-making. The Bible states, "The beginning of wisdom is the fear of the Lord." (Proverbs 9:10) The fear of the Lord produces the greatest possibility any person can ever have in this life. There is no better life than a life lived in the will of the Lord! To put it simply, walking in the fear of the Lord is our advantage to walking in the perfect will of God for our lives. If we fear Him, we will honor and obey His statutes in all things—He will be paramount in our lives. It is easy to see those who walk in the fear of the Lord; their lives are in complete service to His will. Purpose is what drives them. The question we need to ask ourselves is: "Do we understand the fear of the Lord?" The fear of the Lord is different from what many may interpret the word "fear." It is not to be afraid, but it simply means being able to do His will in all things with reverence and joy. The fear of the Lord means following God irrespective of negative circumstances. For the unbeliever, the fear of the Lord is judgment and eternal death, which is eternal separation from God. The fear of the Lord is referential trust. It is awe—it is an understanding of how great God is. Psalms 33:8-9 states, "Let all the earth fear the Lord; let all the inhabitants of the world stand in awe of him. For he spoke and it was done; he commanded, and it stood fast."

The Eyes of Understanding

"I cease not to give thanks for you, making mention of you in my prayers that the God of our Lord Jesus Christ the Father of glory may give unto you the spirit of wisdom and revelation in the knowledge of him. The eyes of your understanding being enlightened; that ye may know what is the hope of his calling, and what the riches of the glory of his inheritance in the saints." (Ephesians 1:16-18)

What are the Eyes of our Understanding? It is when our inner sight becomes open, not the natural sight, but the inner sight of the spirit. When God begins to open our understanding and the inner eyes, what we come to understand will usually contradict what we have always believed or presently believe. The understanding from God will always contradict the view of the world. King Solomon asked God for an understanding heart, which is able to discern the difference between right and wrong. (1 Kings 3:9) God delights to give wisdom and understanding to those who seek it. God responded to Solomon's request for wisdom by promising three different things:

The first was the wisdom Solomon asked for. "I now do according to your word. Behold, I give you a wise and discerning mind, so that none like you has been before you and none like you shall arise after you" (Verse 12) First Kings 4:29-34 records the details of Solomon's wisdom: "And God gave Solomon wisdom and understanding beyond measure, and breadth of mind like the sand of the seashore, so that Solomon's wisdom surpassed the wisdom of Egypt. For he was wiser than all other men, wiser than Ethan the Ezrahite, and Heman, Calcol, and Darda, the sons of Mahol, and his fame was in all the surrounding nations. He also spoke, 3000 proverbs, and his songs were 1005. He spoke of trees, from the cedar that is in Lebanon to the hyssop that grows out of the wall. He spoke also of beasts, and of birds, and reptiles, and fish. And people of all nations came to hear the Wisdom of Solomon, and from all the kings of the earth, who had heard of his wisdom." The second was long life, and the third was riches and glory. All these came as a result of his wisdom and God's support. The eyes of understanding stands out to see what may be perceived as foolish. For example, the death of Jesus on the cross was divine wisdom at work; the devil could not perceive what was happening. God used him to crucify Jesus for the penalty of our sins [this is called the law of substitution in the realm of the spirit]. "If the princes of this world had known they would not have crucified the Lord of glory." (1 Corinthians 2:8)

God had an understanding that could only be seen by Him. The whole creation was in awe when the Son of God was crucified on the cross. "Even the foolishness of God is wiser than men" the Bible says. (1 Corinthians 1:25)

What is understanding?

Understanding is the truth that you are standing under; every one of us operates under a certain measure of truth. Saul, who later became Paul, really believed that he was doing God's work by persecuting the church. He was persecuting the Jews for believing in Jesus. Nevertheless, Jesus appeared to him on his way to Damascus (Acts 9:3-20). This was after he obtained letters from the High Priest to bind those who worshiped this way (believing in Jesus other than following the Law of Moses), as they would call it. Saul/Paul found out the hard way that he had been completely wrong about Jesus, but that didn't stop Jesus from saving him and putting him on a path to change the world. Paul's testimony can help encourage us and show us how we can share the gospel with people who need to hear it. Jesus appeared to him and knocked him to the ground. Now, because of the brilliance of the light of Jesus, he became physically blind, but the Lord opened the eyes of his understanding. After that encounter, Saul became a believer; he preached repentance to both the Jews and Gentiles. The eyes of his understanding were enlightened. It only takes the light of God for one to see who

Jesus is. If you have not seen this Jesus, ask Him to enlighten the eyes of your understanding by His Spirit and pray this prayer with me: "Lord Jesus, come into my heart and change me; forgive my sins and cleanse me by Your blood. I confess with my mouth that Jesus Christ is Lord, and I believe in my heart that God raised Him from the dead. I accept You, Jesus, as my Lord and Savior; I am a new creature in Christ Jesus. Amen." Sometimes before God can get us to understand things, He has to block other means of vision that we've always had. This is not to make us blind, but it is the work on different levels of understanding that we have, by the things we have come to know and see. The only way we can understand the things of God is to allow the Holy Spirit to open up our eyes of understanding about not just Scripture but a lot of other things.

Consciousness

Consciousness is the guide of the soul—Judges and pronounces verdicts upon all we say or do. It is the moral judiciary of the soul. Consciousness does not lay down a law, but warns of the existence of a law. Our consciousness is put within us to tell us about a moral law. There is no rule on how we should conduct our lives, but consciousness convicts us anytime we do wrong. Some have grown up by the golden rule: "Do unto others as you would have them, do unto you." (Matthew 7:12) The golden rule is a principle which teaches about ethics. It is a rule that aims to help people how to behave towards each other—in a way that is morally good. Essentially, the golden rule exhorts people to imagine any interaction from the other person's perspective—considering how they would want to be treated if they were in such a position and then treat the other person accordingly.

Consciousness is different from the golden rule; it provides a witness for our soul. A witness to make sure we make good choices. For believers, the Holy Spirit takes the role of conscienceless in the realm of the heart. Many call this the anointing within. (1 John 2:27) Being led by the inward witness is the primary way God leads all His children. For others who are not born again, God has made a provision for you— to be led by the witness of consciousness.

Consciousness is different from the leading of the Spirit of God. Consciousness only tells you about right and wrong, but the witness of the Spirit goes a long way:

- It tells you when there is a problem ahead.

- It warns you when you are about to make a wrong investmentdecision.

- It tells you when it's time to pray. It is good to be led by ourconsciousness, but much better to be led by the Holy Spirit in the inward part of our hearts. Consciousness will not tell you about the future; however, the inward witness of the Spirit will tell you all things: past, present and future.

Wrong conscience or a dead conscience

It is possible for one to have a dead conscience—this happens when we continue to avoid the voice of consciousness time and time again. The result is that consciousness will now be infiltrated by demons to call good evil and evil good. Just imagine, the very thing that is supposed to guide us on how we should conduct life becomes defile, to a point of misleading us. Many deny to be led by their consciousness and end up been used by Satan himself. Convicting conscience The Bible teaches about a convicting conscience, "They being convicted by their own conscience went out one by one." (John 8:9) Some Pharisees brought a woman caught in the act of adultery to Jesus—they did this to see what Jesus would say should be her punishment.

According to the Law of Moses, "she should be stoned to death." Jesus perceived what they were trying to do. And He pronounced a judgment that was very wise, He said "Let the woman be executed as the Law says; however, her executor should be a righteous man who has not broken any commandment in the Law of Moses." The Bible says they all went on their way because they were convicted by their own sins. (John 8:1-11)

The will of Man The will chooses or rejects things brought before it. God gave men free will—to choose for themselves without Him having to choose for them. This gift is one of the most precious or the most dangerous gifts God gave to men. If it were up to God, He would make all men choose and follow Him, but because of this gift, He is restricted in what He can make men do. He only practices His will upon those who choose to follow Him, and even for these, He lets them make their own choices in all He commands them to do. He leads considering the power of our will. "Choose you this day, whom you will serve, but as for me and my household we shall serve the Lord." (Joshua 24:15) This passage stands out to ask each and every one of us to choose whom we will serve. "Are we going to serve the world and the evil therein? Or we will serve the purpose of God for our lives?" God does not request much from us—just reconciliation and fellowship. Whether we know it or not, man was not created to be an independent entity, but to be a servant of the living God. When we refuse to serve God, we will choose to serve something else. The fact still remains, we all have to serve something or be a slave to something. The confusion we see in the world is for this reason: men were created to serve. Many ask, "Why did God give men free will?" Well, the question of why God gave men free will often comes up in a discussion about the confusion that is happening in the world. Someone will ask "Why is there so much evil in the world?" And the answer is that humans have chosen to do evil things. God is not to blame. The follow-up question will be, "If God knew all the evil things people would choose to do, why He gave us free will?" In the beginning, God gave men a chance to choose between two trees— the "tree of life" and the "tree of the knowledge of good and evil"—this is a convenient way to say "death." Men disobeyed and chose the knowledge of death (sin). I know many will say, "But that was not me!" It is true; however, even to this day God has given everyone of us the same choice He gave to the first man and woman—to choose life or death. I believe we are aware that the sin of Adam and Eve (sinful nature) affects every man that is born to this world except Jesus, because He was not born by the seed of man (sperm), He was the second Adam (1 Corinthians

15:45).

- Choosing life means — accepting Jesus' death on the Cross as our own death (law of substitution) and receiving the life that comes from Him (eternal life)

because He proclaimed. "I am the way, the truth, and the Life, no man comes to the Father but by me." (John 14:6) Jesus is the only One who came out of the dead after dying. That means He defeated death.

• Choosing death means — refusing to accept the One who said "I am the resurrection and the life. The one who believes in me will live, even though they die." (John 11:25) The conclusion is this: the same choice God gave to the angels and the first man and woman emphasizes the reality that we are all tested. We cannot afford to blame Adam while we can make our own choice today, of choosing to follow the begotten of the Father (Jesus) who lives and abides forever and ever. Emotions Emotions are a gift from God to help us relate to Him and one another. There are many emotions in the soul of man; some theories define eight basic emotions, while others say there are more. Emotions are reactions that we experience in response to events or situations. The type of emotions a person experiences is determined by the circumstances that trigger the emotion. For instance, when people don't understand something or are clueless regarding a matter, their emotions become quite or they may not react. But when a person receives good news, an emotion of joy is triggered immediately. Does this mean there is a relationship between the understanding of man and emotions? I believe there is! Emotions are a vital part of who we are, but they can be complicated and downright confusing at times. Dealing with our emotions biblically is not bypassing what someone is going through, but rather helping them take the truth and apply it to their current situation. If anger is triggered and I tell you to calm down, chances are you might come down. So the journey to emotional health is knowing what your emotions are and talking about them to others and God. The Bible states that any emotion should be brought in prayer to God. Philippians 4:6-7 states "Be careful for nothing; but in everything in prayer and supplication with thanksgiving let your request be made known unto god.

And the peace of God, which passes all understanding, shall keep your hearts and minds through Christ Jesus." When we bring our concerns to God, He allows His peace and guidance to come upon us, strengthening us in all situations. Second Corinthians 10:5 also agrees with Philippians 4, encouraging believers to cast down every thought against God's knowledge that triggers negative emotions. Positive Emotions "But the fruit of the Spirit is love, joy, peace, longsuffering, gentleness, goodness, faith, meekness, temperance: against such there is law." (Galatians 5:22-23) These are positive emotions shared by the Holy Spirit upon our hearts. These emotions tender the need for believers to walk in the love of God and let our light shine unto the world. Negative Emotions Negative emotions are there to keep us from enjoying the blessings of God. Fear is the most common emotion that hinders people from enjoying what God has made available in Christ Jesus. "Blessed be God and Father of our Lord Jesus Christ who has blessed us with all spiritual blessings in the heavenly places in Christ Jesus." (Ephesians 1:3) Fear is the common feeling that can hold our emotions hostage; fear has a way of telling us a false story, and many tend to meditate upon what fear displays in their minds. But the Bible states, "For God has not given us the Spirit of fear, but of power, love, and a sound mind." (2 Timothy 1:7) How can people have a sound mind when fear has taken hold of their emotions? By prayer and supplication with thanksgiving, they should make their request known to God.

Types of Emotions

- Adoration.
- Admiration.
- Anxiety.
- Awe.
- Aesthetic appreciation.
- Awkwardness.
- Calmness.
- Confusion.
- Craving.
- Disgusting.
- Empathetic pain.

- Boredom.
- Envy.
- Entrancement.
- Horror.
- Interest.
- Joy.
- Romance.
- Sadness.
- Satisfaction.
- Amusement.

Memory

Memory is the fundamental power of the mind. Memory is the mental capacity for storing knowledge of ideas and events. Everything that happens within our physical experience—bodily condition and future manifestations—is a transmission through the human mind to our memory. We must train our memory to be active in good thinking. Mental exercise is important for brain health. Physical exercise increases oxygen to our brain and reduces the risk for disorders that lead to memory loss. Exercise also enhances the effects of helpful brain cells and reduces stress hormones.

Mind of man

The mind is a precious gift of the soul of man. As we have discussed previously, the mind works as the connecter between the spiritual and the physical through its diverse abilities. The mind is a doorway to the soul and spirit. This means the mind is a field, and it can accept all types of seeds (good and bad) the word "seed" means communication or words. Every word transmitted to the mind has the capacity to grow if neglected by the receiver. We have the responsibility to gate what comes into our minds because the mind has abilities to create our realities. Our actions are a direct result of our thoughts. If your thoughts are downward, your life will move in that direction. And if your thoughts are upward, your life will be upward in the natural. The Bible states, "As a man thinks in his heart so is he." (Proverbs 23:7) Many people's problems are a result of their wrong thinking. Satan fights our minds by projecting evil thoughts into our minds. But we can choose to reject his thoughts through a process called casting down imaginations (2 Corinthians 10:5). There is something about these arguments; they seem to deny what the Word of God says belongs to us. They are trying to make us deny God's power. Thoughts are not independent, and we should be careful of all the thoughts that come into our minds because thoughts carry much significance for our lives and outcomes. The effect of sin on the mind of man Sin has so affected the mind that the Word of God says, "Do not be conformed to this world, but be ye transformed by the renewal of your mind, that ye may prove what is that good, and acceptable, and perfect, will of God." (Romans 12:2) We can only renew our minds by studying the Word of God and meditating upon it. (Joshua 1:8) When one comes to Christ in repentance, their spirits gets born again (2 Corinthians 5:17), but the soul is getting saved by the process of reading the Word of God (renewing the mind).

- Sin has made man's mind defiled and empty. Man is moreconcerned with pleasure and enjoyment than principles and higher truths.

- Sin has made man's mind prejudiced and dishonest.

Chapter 2

Spirit of Man

Heart of Man

"A good man out of the good treasure of his heart brings forth good things, and an evil man out of the evil of the heart brings forth evil things. For out of the abundance of the heart the mouth speaks." (Luke 6:45)

The heart of man is the organ for the spiritual life. Both God and Satan are after the heart. It is the throne of our lives; whoever influences the heart can change one's life. The heart is the subconscious mind of man. The heart has come to stand for the centre of the moral, spiritual, and intellectual life. The Bible states, "For as he thinks in his heart, so is he" (Proverbs 23:7). By reading this passage, the question we need to ask ourselves is, "How are the thoughts of my heart?" As long as we are here on earth, we ought to study the areas of the heart to understand ourselves better. God uses our spirit as a candle to peep into the inward part of our hearts. God is conscience of what is in the inward part of our hearts. God tests the heart of each and every one of us. He's interested in knowing what will come from there. The current state of our life is consistent with the state of our heart. God is concerned about the health of our hearts; the Lord Jesus reveals to us that the heart of man outside of God is wicked.

"For out of the heart proceed evil thoughts, murders, adulteries, fornications, thefts, false witness, and blasphemies: These are the things which defile." (Matthew 15:19-20) How can the heart of man be righteous and do well to please God? Well, God has promised to give us a new heart when we come to Him in repentance. "I will give you a new heart, and put a new spirit in you; I will remove a heart of stone and give you a heart of flesh [a heart that is right with God]." (Ezekiel 36:36) The stony heart is removed from us by the circumcision of the blood of Jesus on the Cross. "In him, you were also circumcised with a circumcision not performed by human hands. Your whole self ruled by flesh was put off when you were circumcised by Christ" (Colossians 2:11). In the Old covenant, Abraham was told to circumcise his children after eight days of birth (Genesis 17:12). This was to continue from generation to generation. However, in Christ, this is different; we are circumcised from the heart, not the skin, and by so doing, we are adopted into the covenant of Abraham in the spirit. Abraham becomes our father through Christ Jesus. God asks for our hearts "My son, give me your heart, and let your eyes delight in my ways." (Psalms 23:26) Giving God our heart means total surrender to His will and mandates for our lives. God wants us to surrender all to Him. Nowadays, it's hard for men to give themselves to God; men are in a quest for something other than God. We are chasing after whatever the world is selling to us.

God has become some old, fantastic story of the Bible. Men want money and all the pleasures the world has to give. Once God owns the heart, He is able to guide and direct us in every area of our life. The opening scripture says, "Give me your heart, and let your eyes delight in my ways." It starts with giving God the heart. How do we give our hearts to God?

• Acknowledging the need for salvation in Christ Jesus. This isthe first step in becoming a follower of Christ: acknowledging that we are sinners in need of a savor. Jesus took our sins on the Cross and offers His righteousness to all who will submit to Him.

• After we acknowledge our sins, we must confess them with ourmouth and ask God for forgiveness and repentance.

• We not only confess, but we confess believing with our heartthat God is faithful to forgive us and cleanse us of all unrighteousness.

• Pursuing a divine relationship with Christ. We do this byengaging in prayers, reading the Word and following what the Word says.

• Call upon the name of the Lord. "Those that call upon thename of the Lord shall be saved." (Romans 10:13) The name of the Lord is a strong tower, and those who run to it find salvation. We find salvation in the name of the Lord. We find salvation when we surrender our hearts to the Lord.

David a man after God's own heart

David is described as a man after God's own heart (1 Samuel 13:14). To understand why David is described this way, we must first look at the circumstances that preceded this declaration from the Lord. Saul was the first God-appointed king of Israel. He was known for his courage and generosity. He was tall and striking in appearance. At first, Saul did well. But things changed when he disobeyed the command from God. God had commanded him, "Go and attack the Amalekites and completely destroy everything they have. Do not spare them. Kill men and woman, infants and nursing babies, oxen and sheep, camels and donkeys." (1 Samuel 15:3) Saul's army attacked and were given victory by the Lord but decided to take the spoil. This was wrong because God had commanded him to "destroy" everything, but he reserved some animals for burnt offering to the Lord. Saul was a fighter for the Lord. One day, while on the battle field, his army was attacked and afraid. Instead of waiting for Samuel to arrive and make a burnt offering to God, Saul took matters into his own hands and made the offering himself. This was wrong because:

- He had been commanded to wait seven days, and this had beenconfirmed by appointed signs.

- He chose to be impatient and disrupted God's plan by hisdisobedience.

- When Samuel came and called him out for this disobedience,instead of taking responsibility for his actions, he made excuses. This disobedience was the beginning of Saul's fall.

The prophet said to him, "Does the Lord delight in burnt offerings and sacrifices as much as in obeying the Lord? To obey is better than sacrifice." (1 Samuel 15:22) Because of his disobedience, lack of faith, and refusing to trust in the Lord, Saul was rejected by the Lord, and David was chosen. David was not as Saul David was a child whom God chose for himself; he did not come from a prominent family. He was just a boy, who used to tend his father's sheep, but the Lord knew his heart and what he could do long before David had any idea what the future had in store for him.

David's faith

David had faith in God when he fought the man known to be Goliath. It took courage to face a sword-wielding giant with nothing but a sling and some rocks. David was sent by his father to the battle field, to check how his brothers were doing—this was after forty days. His father gave him food to give to them. Upon arrival, David saw the Philistine giant (Goliath) making fun of the name of the Lord, the God of Israel, challenging and trampling underfoot the name of the Lord. David became convicted in his heart to do something. David could have remembered how the Lord gave him strength to defeat the lion and the bear in the wilderness. He asked, "What will be given to the man who will defeat this Philistine hero?" His older brother tried to rebuke him, but David persisted in knowing the reward for defeating Goliath. When he knew, he went to fight the Philistine hero. When Goliath saw David, he asked, "I'm I a dog?" Goliath became angry and cursed David by his gods. David answered him back, saying, "This entire assembly will know that the Lord does not save by sword and by spear; for the battle is the Lord's, and He will hand you over to us!" and also said "You come to me with a shield and a sword, I come to you in the name of the Lord the God of the armies of Israel." (1 Samuel 17:45) David attacked the Philistine with his sling, and he hit him in the middle of his forehead, and Goliath fell face down. David went and finished him with his sword (Goliath sword). When the Philistines saw their hero lying there dead, they ran away, and the Israelites pursued them (1 Samuel 17:47). David had faith and trusted the Lord; he knew the Lord would give him victory. Saul did not trust the Lord, but David trusted the Lord, and he knew God will not leave him nor forsake him (Deuteronomy 31:6).

David was Merciful

After Saul knew God had rejected him for his disobedience and had chosen David to be the new king, he sought to kill him. But David could not fight the Lord's chosen king even after God had rejected Saul. In pursue for David, Saul came into a cave where David and his men were hiding, and he slept. When David saw him, he could have killed him, knowing exactly that Saul was there to kill him (1 Samuel 24:114); David had mercy on Saul and did not kill him. David honored God's chosen king; he knew he was the next king but waited for the right time.

David's Humility

After God had made David king and greatly blessed him, David maintained his humility. David had immense success but never gloried in himself; he always gave God the glory. He knew the passage that says, "My son put your trust in the Lord, and never lean on your own strength." (Proverbs 3:5) David continued to honor and served the Lord in faithfulness. Even in times of warfare, he would seek the Lord for guidance. David was a man of integrity David admitted when he was wrong and took responsibility for his mistakes, which was a sign of his deep regret. David had committed adultery with Bathsheba and killed her husband to try and hide his sin, but the prophet Nathan came to him and told him that the Lord had told him what he had done. David was sorry for what he had done; he confessed and found repentance in God. God was merciful and restored him. God did not give up on David. God is always willing to forgive those who will humble themselves and seek His forgiveness. Sure mercies of David "Thus says the Lord; If ye can break my covenant of the day, and my covenant of the night, and that there should not be day and night in their season; Then may also my covenant be broken with David my servant, that he should not have a son to reign upon his throne; and with the Levites." (Jeremiah 33:19-22) David is the only person God gave special mercies to, but the question is, "What does the Bible mean when it speaks of the sure mercies of David?" (Isaiah 55:3). David was faithful to the commandments and the instructions of God; he always judged fairly in his kingdom, he never disregarded the poor and the needy, but ruled God's people as God would if He were physically present here on earth. Because of this, God chose his lineage to be the one Jesus Christ, His Son, will come from. God promised to provide forgiveness, cleansing, and salvation through Jesus Christ. It is based on this promise God made to David that his descendants would reign over His people forever and that God's mercy would not depart from them. "God is described as the tower of salvation for his king, showing mercy to David and his descendants forever." (2 Samuel 22:51) Key of David Revelations 3:7 reads, "To the angel of the church in Philadelphia write: these are the words of him who is holy and true, who holds the key of David." This account reveals of the key of David. This key indicates kingship and authority; therefore, having the key of David would give one control of David's domain—Jerusalem is the city of David and the city God chose as His dwelling place forever (Psalms 132:13). The fact that in Revelations 3:7, Jesus holds this key shows that He is the fulfillment of the covenant God made with David, the ruler of the New Jerusalem. The New Jerusalem shall descend to earth (in Jerusalem), and Jesus will reign from there as King—in the new Heaven and the new Earth.

Law of the Spiritual

The theater of God's display is the heart. God is spirit; we must expect Him to operate from our hearts. This means we must be attentive to all the movements of the Holy Spirit upon our hearts (1 John 2:27) The Holy Spirit will not always speak to us audibly, but He will provide witnesses in the inward part of our hearts regarding every situation we should be careful of. The language of the spirit is:

- Knowing — this happens when we get a witness by the Spirit. We know something, but there was no one who told us.

- Sight — this happens in dreams and trances, or God gives a quick sight (in the mind) and understanding of what we have seen.

• Signs — when we lose our peace. This is a sign that something is not right. We respond as Jesus did before crucifixion (Matthew 26:38-39). He entered into deep prayers.

What is the purpose of Man

Men can know the true meaning of their existence only by understanding who they are in relation to God's creation of mankind as a whole. They need to see how they fit into God's great picture of humanity, which He designed and then constructed when the world began. The first thing we must realize is that there is a distinction between being man and being male or female, and that each has unique purposes for being. What do I mean by this? The account of Creation in the first two chapters of Genesis reveals the essential difference. Genesis 1 is a declaration chapter. It declares what God did in Creation. Genesis 2 is an explanation chapter. It explains how God accomplished His act of Creation and shows how the creation of man relates to the creation of man's two physical manifestations: male and female. In Genesis 1:26–28, we read, then God said, "Let us make man in our image, in our likeness, and let them rule ["have dominion" NKJV] over the fish of the sea and the birds of the air, over the livestock, over all the earth, and over all the creatures that move along the ground." So God created man in his own image, in the image of God He created him; male and female He created them. God blessed them and said to them, "Be fruitful and increase in number; fill the earth and subdue it." The first thing we learn from this passage is that man was made in the image of God. When God made man, He essentially drew man out of Himself, so that the essence of man would be just like Him. Since "God is Spirit" (John 4:24), He created man as spirit. Spirit is eternal. Man was created as an eternal being, because

God is eternal. It is important to recognize that we are not yet talking about male and female. It was mankind that God created in His image. Man is spirit, and spirits have no gender. The Bible never talks about a male or female spirit. What was the reason God created mankind in His image? He didn't create any of the animals or plants in His image. He didn't even make angels in His image. Man is the only being of God's creation that is like Him.

To Be His Offspring

God created mankind for relationship with Himself— to be His family, His offspring, spiritual children of God. The nature of God is to love and to give. Since "God is love" (1 John 4:8, 16), He wanted a being who could be the object of His love and grace. He wanted man to be the recipient of all that He is and all that He has. The fact that man was created in God's image is an awesome revelation about our relationship to Him. God desired children who would be like Himself. Yet He didn't just desire it, then walk away without doing anything about it. He conceived His desire and made it a reality. He became pregnant with what He was desiring. Once God conceived, He began to prepare for the birth or creation of man. Before there was anything at all on the earth, there was God, and God was pregnant with us. What do we call a woman who is pregnant? Expectant. God was in expectation of man's birth, so right away He began to prepare a—nursery for His children, even before there was any physical evidence of His offspring. God's desire for His children caused Him to create the universe in preparation for their arrival. Let me tell you what we've been taught, and it's not biblical. We've been taught that God created the universe, and then He decided to make man. That's not the way it happened. God first decided to make man, and that was the reason for the creation of the world. When my wife and I were expecting our first child, we had the nursery fixed up before the baby arrived. I remember the day it was finished and we stood looking at the whole thing. We had thoroughly cleaned the room. We had the new crib, pillow, sheets, powder, baby oil, diapers, baby food, and everything else all ready. We had little pictures on the walls. There was no baby, but everything the baby would need and use was ready. Then we stepped back, looked at the room, and said, this is good. What were we doing? Preparing.

That's exactly what God was doing in Genesis 1 when He made the world in preparation for the creation of man. Just as a new baby is at the center of his parents' thoughts, mankind was and is at the center of God's thoughts. The wonder of this idea struck King David one day. He said, "When I consider your heavens, the work of your fingers, the moon and the stars, which you have set in place, what is man that you are mindful of him, the son of man that you care for him?" (Ps. 8:3–4). David asked God, in effect, Why are you thinking only about us? Although the psalm doesn't give us God's answer, I think His reply would be, —Every time you see the moon and the stars, and everything else I've created, I want you to know that all that exists because of you. We are so important to God that He created the entire universe for us. Not only that, He created it with great care to make sure we had the best environment in which to live. Everything God created keeps everything else in balance. For example, when He made our solar system, He created the sun to be a light for us, and then He carefully placed the planets around it. I can imagine God making adjustments so that the solar system would be just right for us. I see Him pushing the earth out a bit, then saying, No, it's too close to the sun. That's too hot. Let's pull it back a little. Now it's too cold. They'll freeze. Ah, this is just right. The conditions are perfect. The baby will do fine. Then I imagine Him saying, children like colors, so let's cause some vivid flowers to spring up from the ground. That's a beautiful rose; they'll like that. Let's put some colors on the fish, too. Now, we've already created the sunset, but let's make the ozone layer run right past the light so that it changes color. Let the light come through the atmosphere and the stratosphere, so that when it hits them it will turn purple, yellow, blue, and pink. I see Him thinking about man's future physical needs. Now we must have a lot of food for the baby. We'll need some fruits and vegetables. We also need to separate the salt water from the fresh, so that the baby can drink. Now—everything is in order. The nursery is ready! I submit to you that man is the reason for the universe. I didn't say man is the center of it. Humanists say that man is the center of the universe. That is wrong. God is the center of everything. He "[upholds] all things by the word of his power" (Heb. 1:3 KJV). It is He who is the center of life. Everything He created and every movement of our being exists in Him. Yet because we are His offspring, He created the universe just for us. When God finished creating the world, He called everything good. (See Genesis 1:4–25.) I believe He said this because everything was ready. It was after God called the physical world good that He said, "Let us make man" (v. 26). What's so interesting about this is that the heavens and the earth were created first because of their purpose. Some people might say, well, if the heavens and earth were created first, does that mean that they are more important than man? No. They were just leading up to the advent of man. Their purpose was to be a perfect environment for God's children. When my wife and I were getting the nursery ready, we had the crib, powder, and all the other material things in the room first. Did that mean they were more important than the baby? No. Those things were there only because of the baby. The same is true concerning man's relationship to the physical world. Ephesians 1:4 explains the order of priority in this way: "For he chose us in him before the creation of the world" (emphasis added).

To Have Fellowship with Him

Another reason man was created in God's image was to have fellowship with Him, like a close family relationship. The only reason man can have this fellowship with God is that God made man to be spirit, just as He is Spirit. "God is spirit, and his worshipers must worship in spirit and in truth" (John 4:24). Although God is the Creator, He has always emphasized that He is man's Father. It wasn't His desire to be primarily thought of by man as an awesome God or a "consuming fire" (Deut. 4:24). Although at times it is difficult for our religious minds to grasp this concept, God wants us to approach Him as a child would a loving father. God and humanity were made for one another. That is why, no matter how many relationships you have or how many gifts you buy for others, in the end, you aren't going to be satisfied until you love God. God must have the primary place in your life. Your love was designed to be fulfilled in Him.

To Manifest His Nature

God created man in His image so that man could also reflect His character and personality. When God created man, heaven and earth stood in awe of this amazing being who manifested the Creator's very nature and reflected His glory. Consider this remarkable verse in Psalm 82: "I said, „You are gods, and all of you are children of the Most High"" (v. 6 NKJV). This verse is speaking of mankind. It calls us "gods" and "children of the Most High." Why are we called little gods? It is because as children of the Most High God, we have His nature and share His purposes. Physically, we are children of men, but spiritually, we are children of God. Two foundational aspects of God's character are love and light, and man is meant to exhibit these qualities. However, man's being made in God's image does not mean that man can reveal these qualities apart from Him. Man was always meant to reveal God's nature in the context of being continually connected to Him in fellowship. First John 4:16 says, "Whoever lives in love lives in God, and God in him," and Proverbs 20:27 says, "The spirit of man is the candle of the Lord" (KJV). This means that when you have fellowship with God, you reflect His light. You show the nature of God, for "God is light; in him there is no darkness at all" (1 John 1:5). God also created man to demonstrate His wisdom and the goodness of His precepts.

This purpose is part of God's eternal plans, and it culminated in the coming of Christ Jesus and the birth of the church: His intent was that now, through the church, the manifold wisdom of God should be made known to the rulers and authorities in the heavenly realms, according to his eternal purpose which he accomplished in Christ Jesus our Lord. (Eph. 3:10–11)

To Share His Rule

God said, “Let us make man in our image, in our likeness, and let them rule [“have dominion” NKJV]” (Gen. 1:26, emphasis added). Man was created to share God‘s authority. God never wanted to rule by Himself. Love doesn‘t think in those terms. You can always tell a person who is full of love. He doesn‘t want to do anything for his purposes alone. A selfish person wants all the glory, all the credit, all the recognition, all the attention, all the power, all the authority, all the rights, and all the privileges. But a person of love wants others to share in what he has. Note that the word “man” in Genesis 1:26 refers to the spirit-being created in God‘s image. The purpose of dominion was given to man the spirit. This was before the creation of male and female, which we will discuss in more detail shortly. Therefore, spiritually, both male and female have the same responsibility toward the earth because rule was given to the spirit-man, which resides in both of them. The account of Creation reveals an interesting fact that we often overlook today. God didn‘t create man for heaven. He created man for the earth. God is the Ruler of heaven, and He made man to express His authority on earth. He said, —I want what‘s happening in heaven to happen in the created world; I want My rule to extend to another realm, but I don‘t want to do it directly. I want man to share My rule. The plan of Creation was this: as God ruled the unseen realm in heaven, man would rule the visible realm on earth, with God and man enjoying continual communion through their spiritual natures. God said to man, in essence, —Let Me rule through you so you can appreciate, enjoy, and share in rulership and know how it feels to be 'little gods.' It's important to realize that man was created not only for fellowship with God but also with a responsibility to carry out. I want to emphasize this point because sometimes people use their worship of God as an excuse for negligence in other areas of their lives. They say, —I was created only to love the Lord, worship the Lord, and praise the Lord. These things are good and necessary. However, you can't spend all your time in the sanctuary worshiping, praising, and singing. There comes a time when you have to carry out your responsibility to demonstrate what your relationship with the Lord means in terms of living and ruling in the world. Man has been given the freedom to exhibit creativity while governing the physical earth and all the other living things that dwell in it. The earth is to be ruled over, taken care of, fashioned, and molded by beings made in the image of their Creator. In this way, man is meant to reflect the loving and creative Spirit of God.

To Expand the Family Business

We also need to understand that when God created man to share His authority, it was in the context of man's relationship to Him as His offspring. God didn't create man to be a servant but to be a son who is involved in running the family business. This was His plan for mankind from the beginning. He has always wanted His children to help Him fulfill His purposes. This means that God doesn't want man to work for Him; He wants man to work with Him. The Bible says that we are "God"s fellow workers" (2 Cor. 6:1) or "workers together with him"

(KJV). In the original Greek, "fellow workers" means those who —cooperate, who —help with, who —work together. It‘s common to hear people say, —I‘m working for Jesus. If you are working for Jesus, you are still a hired hand. When you understand the family business, then you become a worker alongside Christ.

To Rely on the Father for Personal Needs

What are some of the implications of our being God‘s children, working in His business? First, we don‘t have to worry about our day-to-day living expenses. If your father and mother owned a prosperous business, and they put you in the business to run it, should you wonder where you will get food to eat? Should you wonder where you will get water to drink? Should you wonder where you‘re going to get clothes to wear? No, you are family, and you are going to be provided for. If you are hired to work in the business only as an employee, then you don‘t know the company‘s true financial condition. In addition, if you want more money, you have to ask for a raise. You have to work hard to receive a bonus. You have to impress the boss so that you can get just a little increase in salary. You may also live in fear of being fired. However, if you are a son, you know just how well the company is doing. In God‘s company, there‘s always plenty of provision to go around, and you can rely on that with confidence. Jesus said, "Do not worry, saying, "What shall we eat?"or "What shall we drink?" or "What shall we wear?" For the pagans run after all these things, and your heavenly Father knows that you need them. But seek first his kingdom and his righteousness, and all these things will be given to you as well. (Matt. 6:31–33) Jesus didn‘t say, —The boss knows that you need these things. He said, —Your Father knows that you need these things. We can trust our Father, the wealthy Businessman, to provide for all our needs.

To Rely on the Father for Kingdom Needs When Jesus knew that His earthly ministry was about to end and that He would be crucified, resurrected, and then return to His heavenly Father, He talked to His disciples about their role in advancing the family business on earth. "I no longer call you servants, because a servant does not know his master"s business. Instead, I have called you friends, for everything that I learned from my Father I have made known to you" (John 15:15). What was Jesus' reason for calling His disciples His friends? He said, in effect, —The servant doesn't know what the boss is doing. I call you friends because I have told you everything the Father has revealed to Me. Think about how large and prosperous God's business is. It is so big that God says He can supply all your needs (Phil. 4:19). I don't think that in this context He is referring to your smaller needs, such as a house, a car, clothes, or food. Remember that He told us we don't even have to ask for those things. Therefore, He must be talking about leads for further investment for the purpose of expanding the company business. He is saying, in essence, —The company has so much collateral that My children never have to worry about materials for further investment. I believe that if we will get busy spreading the company's influence and building its interests, our access to resources will be unclogged. (See Matthew 6:33.) God created man to be His offspring and to work in His business, and He has all the resources we need to fulfill this purpose.

To Execute His Righteous Judgment

Man was created in God's image for yet another reason: to execute His righteous judgment. In all the prophecies about the Messiah, especially in Isaiah, Jeremiah, and Daniel, you will find that this was also the main purpose for Christ's coming to earth. It was the result of His life, ministry, death, and resurrection. All these things were connected to His fulfilling His purpose of executing righteous judgment on the earth. The reason this is also the purpose of man is that it is God's intention that we rule the earth through the Spirit of Christ. Recall that, through man, God desires to extend His rule from the unseen to the seen. He wants to expose His character, nature, principles, precepts, and righteous judgment to the visible world. Even though the fall of man brought humanity out from under God's purposes, Christ redeemed us so we could be restored to His original plans for us.

Dominion over the earth, including exercising righteous judgment, is not a temporary but an eternal assignment from God to man. Because of the Fall, when we die, our spirits will separate from our bodies, and we will go to be with God in heaven. Again, it was never God's intention that man would work in heaven. Even though in our spiritual growth and development we will learn to have dominion over spiritual as well as physical things (see 1 Corinthians 6:3), God gave man the earth to rule. Since God's purposes never change, He made provision in His plan of redemption for man to fulfill that purpose. God made us a promise. He said that when we come to the head office (heaven), we will stay there only for a while. There will come a Day when our bodies will be resurrected and rejoined with our spirits, so that He can send us back to finish the job. (See 1 Corinthians 15:42–44, 52–53; Isaiah 65:17.) If you are finding it hard to take all this in, read the book of

Revelation. God keeps on talking about thrones, reigning with Him, and ruling with Him. The reason we will reign is that Jesus came to bring righteous judgment back to the earth.

He came to bring it back to where it was supposed to be in the first place. That has always been God's purpose for man. God made you a manager, and He always fulfills His eternal purposes. He isn't going to raise you from the dead just to live with Him forever. He's going to raise you from the dead so that you can get on with your work. That's why the Scripture says that when Jesus returns to earth and we are resurrected, we will reign with Him (Rev. 5:10.) Reign means what? To have dominion, to administrate.

Created Male and Female

Therefore, God created man so that He could have someone to love, someone who would work with Him in His purposes for the earth. Yet the earth is a physical entity, and man is spirit. The earth needed someone with a physical body to live in it and take care of it. God knew this would be necessary, and that is a primary reason He created the male and the female. "So God created man in his own image, in the image of God he created him; male and female he created them" (Gen. 1:27). After God created man, He placed him in two physical —houses: male and female. This means that man the spirit exists within every male and every female. All of us— males and females alike— are man. The essence of both male and female is the resident spirit within them, called —man. Genesis 5:1–2 says, "When God created man, he made him in the likeness of God. He created them male and female and blessed them. And when they were created, he called them [together] „man."" Why did God take man, who is spirit, and put him in two separate physical entities rather than just one? It was because He wanted man to fulfill two distinct purposes. We'll explore the significance of this fact in more detail in coming chapters. For now, we need to remember that the spirit man has no gender and that, in order to fulfill His eternal purposes, God used two physical forms to express the spiritual being made in His image. Therefore, whether you are male or female, the person who lives inside you—the essential you—is the spirit man. Although males and females have differences, they are of the same essence. Since human beings fellowship with God and worship Him through their spirits, this means that men and women both have direct spiritual access to God and are individually responsible to Him.

"Created" versus "Made"

Genesis 1:26–27 implies that the process through which God created man was different from the process through which He produced the male and female. We can think of the distinction in this way: God created man, but He made male and female. The words for "made" in verse 26 and "created" in verse 27 are different words in the Hebrew. "Make" comes from asah, which means to form out of something that is already there. "Created" comes from bara, which means to form out of nothing. These verses say that God created man in His own image, but that God also made man. God used both of these words in reference to how He brought man into existence. In effect, He was saying,

—I will both create him and make him. I will create him out of nothing and I will make him out of something. Recall that God created the spirit-man out of His own being rather than out of anything from the physical world. Man was not created from matter; man came out of God's Spirit. Therefore, the part of man that was made from —nothing came out of God. God spoke him into existence, similar to the way in which He spoke, "„Let there be light,"̈ and there was light" (Gen. 1:3). Yet when God made male and female, He used material from the physical world that He had already created. Recognizing this distinction is critical to understanding our purpose in the world as both spiritual beings made in God's image and physical beings who carry out man's God ordained purposes in the world. It is also essential to the male's understanding of who he is and how he is meant to relate to the female. We will see the practical

implications of these purposes in the next chapter. Principles

1. Men can know the true meaning of their existence only byunderstanding who they are in relation to God's creation of mankind as a whole.
2. There is a distinction between being man and being male.
3. Mankind was created in the image of God.
4. God created man to be spirit, as He is Spirit.
5. Man was created to be God's offspring, to have fellowship withHim, to manifest His nature, to share His rule, to expand the family business, to rely on the Father for personal needs and for kingdom needs, and to execute God's righteous judgment.

6. After God created man, He placed him in two physical

—houses: male and female.

1. Man—the spirit-man— resides within both male and female.
2. God created man, but He made male and female.
3. God made male and female because He wanted man to fulfill

two distinct purposes on the physical earth. [1]

The spirit of man and what happens after death

"Then the dust will return to the earth as it was, and the spirit will return to God who gave it." (Ecclesiastes 12:7) Many misinterpret this passage and jump to wrong conclusions that it is a reference to righteous souls going to heaven. This context shows this interpretation to be wrong.

It says the spirit of everyone who dies goes back to God who gave it. It is speaking of the life-giving breath God breathed into the nostrils of man. "And breathed into his nostrils the breath of life; and man became a living soul." (Genesis 2:7) The breath of God did two things: it created a soul and made man alive in the natural. What is the meaning of the word "death?"

This life is all too fleeting, and we naturally want there to be something more. But how can we really know what happens beyond the great gulf of death? Death is one of our least favorite topics. It provokes worry and fear about our own well-being, as well as feelings of sadness, regret and loss for family and friends who have died. But we can't ignore death because it is something we all must confront at some point. One reason death causes so much fear, is confusion about what comes next. What really happens after we die? Numerous cultures and religions have proposed answers to that question. The scores of explanations can be summarized by three basic options:

• There is no afterlife, and death is literally the end of life forall eternity. This is the answer commonly proposed by atheists. According to this explanation, we should live life to its fullest, perhaps do something to help make the world a better place and prepare to die because after that there is nothing more.

• After death, humans are reincarnated into a different kind oflife-form, moving up or down the hierarchy of existence based on how they live. This view is often held by adherents of Eastern religions.

• The typical Christian belief is that after death, the human soulcontinues to live in an alternate state. Though specifics vary, the most common beliefs are that the soul either ascends to the reward of heaven after death or descends to punishment in hell. Oddly enough, this teaching originated long before Christianity and is, in fact, the belief of many ancient religions and cultures—including those in Babylon, Egypt, Greece and Rome. The last two belief systems are still the most common. We want to believe that our loved ones—and we ourselves— are not lost for all eternity after death. We want there to be a greater purpose for our existence that extends beyond the grave. Billions of people have lived and died throughout history; there has to be an answer to where they all are now. But if we are to come to any meaningful and true understanding about what happens after death, we must consider what source we will use as the basis for our understanding. Is human reason alone adequate to provide a clear, believable, universally accepted understanding of what happens after death? If not, is there any reliable, authoritative source that has the ability to help us understand a matter that lies completely outside of human experience? It is logical that the giver of life would be the ultimate source for understanding what happens when life ends and what the entire purpose of human existence is. The only viable source for answers to these questions is the being that created life (God). He has not hidden the answers away in some obscure place, but has shared them with those who are willing to turn to Him for understanding. He has revealed the truth to us plainly, beginning in the first verse of His Bible: "In the beginning God created the heavens and the earth" (Genesis 1:1). A few verses later, we read: "Then God said, 'Let Us make man in Our image'" (verse 26). Since God created life, He can reveal its purpose and what happens when human life ends. The Bible contradicts what is most believed about life and death. The beliefs listed earlier are myths— none represents the teachings of the Bible.[2]

Death in simple terms means separation, not end of life. The Bible reveals three kinds of death:

- Physical death - the spirit leaving the body. This type of death is common in human society. We are all aware that at some point it will take us, as it does many around the world. "We are confident, I say and willing rather to be absent from the body and be present with the Lord." (2 Corinthians 5:8)

- Spiritual death - separation from God. We are all born spiritually dead (separated) because of our sinful nature. But we are reconciled with God by the forgiveness of sins through Christ Jesus. "And you who were dead in your trespasses and sins, in which you formerly walked according to the course of this world, according to the spirit that now worketh in the children of disobedience." (Ephesians 2:1-2) However, the death of Jesus on the Cross does not automatically reconcile us to God, but the ministry of reconciliation happens when we accepts Jesus into our hearts (Romans 10:9).

• Second death - eternal separation from God. This death is to be avoided at all costs because the second death is unrecoverable This happens if we die before we reconcile with God (John 3:3) "But for the cowardly and unbelieving and abominable and murders and immoral persons and sorcerers, and idolaters and all liars shall have their part in the lake of fire that burns with sulphur and brimstone." (Revelations 21:8)

Chapter 3

Body of Man

The body is the physical structure of man (person) including the bones, flesh, and organs. Every cell of our bodies has a very detailed unique generic code carried by a long molecule called DNA, which instructs the cells to develop, function, grow, survive, and reproduce. It is through our bodies that we can perceive the physical world using five senses—the senses of sight, hearing, taste, smell and touch. The Bible teaches that our bodies are the temple of the Holy Spirit; therefore, it is important for our bodies to be pure. God asks us to give Him our bodies as a living sacrifice, "I beseech you therefore, brethren, by the mercies of God, that ye present your bodies a living sacrifice, holy, acceptable unto God, which is your reasonable service." (Romans 12:1) The scripture speaks of consecration. Paul is trying to let us know that for us to worship or serve God effectively, we have to give our bodies to God as a living sacrifice. Warfare's we encounter in our walk with God have a certain level of consecration for us to be victorious. Consecration in effective priesthood means there is a level we must fast, there is level we must pray, and there is a level we must purify ourselves. God wants our bodies as a burnt offering before His majesty. God does not want the meat of rams and bulls as a burnt offering but our bodies. God wants us to be separated unto Him. A separated individual is a person who lives to please not his own will but the will of the Father. Paul says before God can accept the sacrifice of the body, it has to be holy. The subject of holiness is very important in the kingdom of kings and priests (Revelations 1:6). Israel did not keep the covenants of God in the wilderness. After God led the Israelites out of slavery, He made a covenant with them so they could serve Him as priests. The whole nation, not just one tribe, all the tribes of Israel. "Now therefore, if you will obey my voice indeed, and my covenant, then you shall be a peculiar treasure unto me above all people: for all the earth is mine: and you shall be unto me a kingdom of priests, and a holy nation." (Exodus 19:5-6) This was God's plan for Israel: to be a peculiar treasure unto Him. Israel was going to be a nation that was not going to operate like other nations in the world; they were going to bring the counsel of God to the people of the world. Darkness was going to be arrested if all twelve tribes of Israel were priests of the Most High. They were going to give God the right to come to the earth and disarm darkness. All nations of the world would go there to interact with God. Israel was going to be a place of healing and miracles. They were going to live according to the script or the scrolls in heaven. But things changed after they made a golden calf and worshiped it as their god. God wanted to destroy them (read Exodus 32-1-13). They broke covenant with God, and as a result, God only archived to make one tribe out of twelve tribes to be priests. And God never ceased His plan of making a peculiar nation and a kingdom of priests on earth. When the Lord Jesus came to the earth and paid the price for our redemption, He adopted us to this amazing plan. God has archived His plan of making a kingdom of priests with believers, but this does not mean He has forsaken the Jews. The Jews are the primary people when it comes to the promises of God; they are a nation God chose for Himself. As believers, we must take note of this reality: the Israelites are the first, and then come the Gentiles. God will never forsake the Israelites even though they rejected Jesus as the Messiah. He loves them, and they will be His people forever and ever. "Unto him that loved us and washed us from our sins in his own blood and has made us kings and priests unto God and his Father." (Revelations 1:6) And this is what Peter was trying to let us know in 1 Peter 2:9 when he said, "But ye are a chosen generation, a royal priesthood, and holy nation, peculiar people; who he hath called you out of darkness into his marvelous light." When you read this verse thoroughly, you see that God called us into the same calling He originally had for the Israelites because the prescriptions of the calling are the same: "A royal nation, peculiar people, and a royal priesthood." We have been made a nation unto God, and, "We have received the Spirit of adoption whereby we cry Abba Father." (Romans 8:15) Every man who comes to Jesus for salvations receives this stature in God, to be a priest and a king. The work of priests is to offer up spiritual sacrifices unto God by Christ Jesus. Nowadays, God is sharing us with many things, but originally we are only supposed to live to serve the will of God. God wanted to camp on earth through Israel, but they kept on disobeying and opened this possibility to us, the Gentiles. We are also missing it in some areas of our Christian life. Every believer in this holy nation is supposed to be submitted to God. And God, who is the Lord of the harvest, will now deploy us in the areas of service that are consistent with His kingdom plan. The job description of the believer is to serve God, and service is actually the key to greatness in the kingdom, as Jesus said in Matthew 20:26, "But it shall not be so among you; but whosoever will be great among you, let him be your minister." In consecration, we acknowledge we are God's property, and the only use we have is where the Lord puts us. Where He puts us is where He wants us to function. God has a role for every one of us to play, and that role can only be fulfilled by you because God is telling a unique story in the life of every believer, and the only thing that can make you fulfil that role will require that you are consecrated unto God. There are parts to consecration, and there are systems God has put in place—legal and organic systems—to ensure our submission to Him is a journey of great delight. "What? Know you not that your body is the temple of the Holy Ghost which is in you, which you have of God, and you are not your own? For you are brought with a price: therefore glorify God in your body, and in your spirit, which are God's." (1 Corinthians 6:19-20) If one can successfully commit sin with their body, it is proof they are not aware of the fact that we are not our own; we were bought with a price of the blood of Jesus. This scripture reveals a legal position, and by reason of property law, we are God's possession. We don't have the right to entertain evil thoughts that lead to sin. We must cast them down to the obedience of Christ. Because we are brought with a price, our bodies must glorify God, and our spirits, which are God's property, and being priests doesn't make us consecrated believers. We still have a will of our own to choose what we want to do. Remember, Paul beseeches us to give our bodies to God (Romans 12:1). The reason God wants us consecrated is because of purpose; if we are not consecrated, we can never get to where God wants us to be. There is a place God is taking us in destiny, but we don't have the map of where we are going. We need to please Him for us to get there, and God is pleased by people who do His commandments and will. In the journey with God, everything that happens in our spiritual life matters— every dream, everything He tells us. If God has stopped leading you towards destiny, it means something is not right, and you need to check it; sometimes it might be that you did not obey when He asked you to do something or go somewhere. And sometimes it can be that you are not keeping to the requirements of your consecration.

Another thing that is critical is that we must be willing to serve the will of God. When God created man, He gave man free will, and it takes our willingness to be consecrated believers. We belong to God by legal rights, but God is not like the devil; He does not force us to do His will. So it takes our willingness to serve Him according to the prescribed standard, which is holy living. Our consecration to God is what determines the level of our walk with God. The more sacrifice we give to God in consecration, the greater the power God will commit to us. God means business; He is not compromising. Consecration to God will affect everything we do and how we live our lives because the nation of priests is a fully integrated community of servants who are living to serve the will of God.

What is Consecration?

The reason we consecrate ourselves is that God has taken the first step to purchase us with His blood. Consecration, therefore, is:

- The reasonable response to the gesture of sacrificial love thatwas displayed on the Cross. So Paul is beseeching us in Romans 12:1 to reciprocate the love of Christ on the Cross by giving our bodies to Him as a living sacrifice. There is a love element in consecration.

- Consecration is to be willing to serve the will of God as yournumber one priority in this life. It is giving yourself to the price of the call.

- Consecration is being separated unto God to serve His will.

- Consecration is living a holy life.

- Consecration is denying ourselves to serve God, as Paul said inPhilippians 1:21, "For me to live is Christ." These are the words of a consecrated believer.

The thin line between an accurate Christian and a false Christian is that cry of Paul in begging us by the mercies of God to consecrate unto God by presenting our bodies as a burnt offering.

About the Author

Tumisang Mabe is a believer. He was born again when he was eleven years old after watching a deliverance program by Pastor Tshifhiwa Irene. God used Pastor Irene's program to capture the young boy; however, his conversion did not begin there. Tumisang grew up in a Christian home, where his mom played a very important role that led to his conversion. His mom went with him to church almost every Sunday. Tumisang was a Sunday school learner, and he believes that what he learned in Sunday school translated to his conversion.

Now, while Tumisang was watching Pastor Irene's program, the Pastor was casting out demons from those who attended the crusade; men and women were crawling on the ground while the Pastor was saying "fire." This view caught Tumisang's eye. The boy wondered whether these people were real because, by their reactions, it seemed like it, and he asked himself if people who have not received Christ into their lives, when they die, will burn like those on the television forever and ever. The boy understood that those who do not have Christ in their lives will be in doom's trouble. Immediately, the boy ran to his mom and told her that he wants to receive Jesus into his life because he does not want to go to hell when he dies. From then on, the boy grew up in the knowledge of the Lord.

Tumisang is a New Testament believer, an Apostle called to teach the Word of God. God has given Tumisang the teaching grace to serve the body of Christ. "The calling of a believer is the same as the calling of our father Abraham. God has called us to a distant land through spiritual pathways in search of our eternal inheritance. It is a privilege to be a part of what God is doing on earth, because whatever we do for the Lord here on earth will translate to our eternal rewards in heaven." Tumisang Mabe

Other books by the Author

Warfare of the Mind

"For we wrestle not against flesh and blood, but against principalities and powers, against the rulers of the darkness of this world, against spiritual wickedness in high places." (Ephesians 6:12)

There are two very real worlds at work, physical and spiritual. A careful study of the opening scripture reveals to us that we are in a war. Our warfare is not physical but spiritual. We can ignore the spiritual realm and focus on the natural, but unfortunately, we will lose the war. We need spiritual weapons to fight the warfare of the mind. The mind is a spirit, but it has the capacity to function in the natural through its diverse faculties. The mind is the battlefield of the spiritual realm. The Bible teaches us to be "sober-minded" because the enemy prowls around like a roaring lion seeking whom he may devour (1 Peter 5:8).

The question we need to ask ourselves is: Are we in control of our minds? The Bible states, "Do not be conformed to this world, but be ye transformed by the renewal of your mind." (Romans

12:2) This account reveals to us that it's possible for one to have a mind of this world; however, God wants us to have the mind of Christ. "Let this mind be in you, which was also in Christ Jesus." (Philippians 2:5) We can have the mind of Christ if we choose to follow the directives of the Word of God.

There are two types of spiritual warfare of the mind, defensive and offensive:

- Defensive spiritual warfare - It is a process when demons are launched to cast fiery darts in our minds. "Above all, taking the shield of faith, wherewith ye shall be able to quench all the fiery darts of the wicked." (Ephesians 6:16) How can we defend ourselves from the fiery darts of the enemy? The statement Paul made in the account above reveals to us that there is armor. We need this armor if we are going to be victorious in the warfare of the mind.

- Offensive spiritual warfare - Usually consists of casting down strongholds that have been formed in our minds. Since strongholds are incorrect thinking patterns because of lies, the correct weapon to use is to tear down those thoughts with the truth of God.

Power of the Mind

- The mind has the power to create.

• The mind is a field - it accepts all types of seeds (good or bad).

• Every thought we think is a force and has an effect in

our life, whether good or bad.

• The spiritual realm is a realm of thoughts. Communication is mostly done in the realm of the mind. Spirits (good or bad) can communicate with us through our minds, and then one may think it was them who was thinking whatever was communicated. Or spirits (good or bad) can cast thoughts in our minds to make us believe whatever the spirit is trying to communicate. When seeds in the form of thoughts are cast in our minds, they take time to grow; when we meditate (water the seed) upon a certain thought, we make that thought become a reality in our lives over time. This should make us careful of all seeds that come into our minds. Thoughts are vibrations in the spirit. I repeat - they have the capacity to determine the direction of one's life through a process called meditation.

What is Man

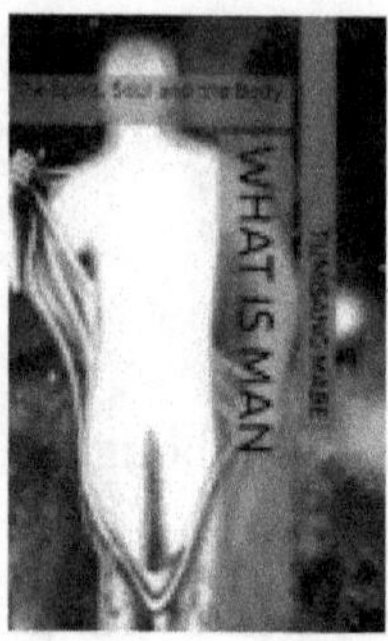

The human being is an extraordinary creature, often regarded as complex synthesis—"beyond" that which is physical. The creation of man is divided into three fundamental aspects: soul, spirit, and body, each playing a pivotal role in essence of human existence.

The soul encompasses the mind, will and emotions, housing various faculties that contribute to the creation of man. Among these faculties we have:

- Imagination — plays a crucial role, enabling us to bring forth ideas into tangible realities or it is what we use to take an idea—something that is non-physical and turn it into something material.

- Perception — another essential faculty, dictates the manner in which we interpret things, uses both conscious and subconscious processes.

- Intuition — serves as an internal guide, often described as the subtle voice that imparts truth.

- Reasoning — facilitates critical thinking, analysis, and comparative evaluation of ideas and events.

- Memory — operates as the repository for past experiences, ideas, and information, allowing for learning and reflection.

Moreover, man is fundamentally a spirit, representing the core dimension of human identity. This spiritual aspect is interface through which men engage with God and the spiritual realm, using the inherent senses of faith, hope, and prayer. The spirit also possesses a subconscious mind.

Man possesses a physical body that interacts with the material world through the five senses of: sight, smell, hearing, taste, and touch. Scientific research indicates that our mental processes, emotions, and will are intricately linked to the body through our endocrine, nervous, and immune systems. Additionally, scripture emphasizes a significant relationship among our physical, emotional, and spiritual well-being. As noted in Proverbs 17:22, "A cheerful heart is good medicine, but a crushed spirit dries up bones."

Priesthood

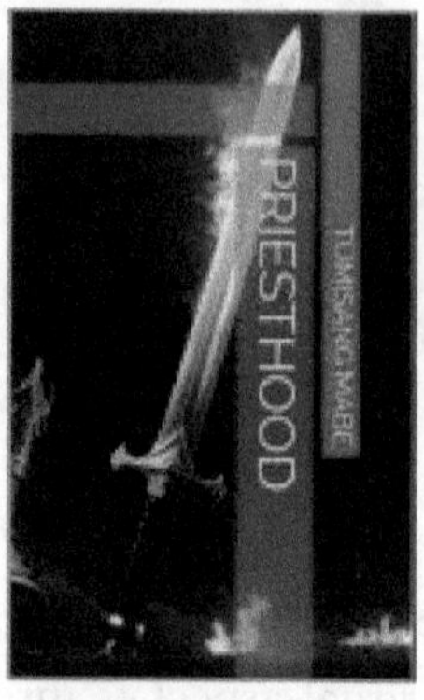

Priesthood is the authority and power of God. In the Old

Testament, the role of a priest was to stand between men and God. In the New Testament, this has changed; men can interact with God by themselves because after Jesus had paid the claims of divine justice on the Cross, the Bible says, "And, behold, the veil of the temple was rent in twain from the top to the bottom; and the earth quake, and the rocks rent" (Matthew 27:51), signifying that every individual has direct access to God and shares the responsibility of ministering to other believers in Christ.

Priesthood Orders

The Epistle to the Hebrews refers to two orders of priesthood: Melchizedek and the Leviticus priesthood. The Leviticus priesthood is the most popular in Scripture; however, the Melchizedek priesthood is considered the "higher priesthood" that incorporates all other priesthoods.

The Functions of Priesthood

Priesthood functions by altars. The thin line between the spiritual and the physical realm makes priesthood significant in connecting the two. Some qualities of a priest include a strong prayer life, the need to read the Word of God, and fellowship with other believers. Our father of faith, Abraham, was a priest and a man of the altar. It takes priesthood and the use of altars for men to secure answers from spirit beings.

The great need of God today is for priests who will pave the way in the spirit (altars) to engage God enough so that He will bring a revival, because the whole society of the human race needs it.

The Rise of the Kingdom of Christ

"Let not your hearts be troubled: ye believe in God, believe also in me. In my Father's house are many mansions: if it were not so, I would have told you. I go to prepare a place for you. And if I go and prepare a place for you, I will come again and receive you unto myself; that where I am, there ye may be also." (John 14:1-3)

The subject of heaven is a very interesting one. Thinking of the fact that we will not only live once, which is here on earth, but there is another life awaiting us called heaven is very good, and it raises a question in each of us: What is heaven like? Who has God once taken there and returned to this life to tell their testimony? Many have shared stories of how they died and went to heaven for a few hours or minutes and came back to this life with a message from God. Many long to see this beautiful place and live in it because of all the amazing stories we have heard in the Word of God and from people who proclaim that the Lord has once taken them there. I will not speak of those testimonies, but I want to speak about what the Word of God says about this place. "And I saw a new heaven and a new earth; for the first heaven and the first earth were passed away: and there was no more sea. And I, John, saw the holy city, New Jerusalem, coming down from God out of heaven, prepared as a bride adorned for her husband. And I heard a great voice out of heaven saying, Behold, the tabernacle of God is with men, and He will dwell with them, and they shall be His people, and God Himself shall be with them and be their God. And God shall wipe away all tears from their eyes; and there shall be no more death, neither sorrow, nor crying, neither shall there be any more pain: for the former things are passed away." (Revelation 21:1-4) It is God's desire to dwell with His creation. He wanted this from the beginning of creation. Sin was the cause that separated the Creator from His creation, which is humanity. Eden was not a location but an extension of heaven here on earth. After sin came, God took Eden back to heaven.

God promised us a new heaven and a new earth, a place where there is no suffering, pain, or Satan. God has an eternal plan, a plan He had from the beginning, and when we study the book of Revelation, we see that God's plan is going to come to pass. If we are to enjoy what God has planned for His creation, it means we must be willing to serve the will of God in all circumstances.

In one of the testimonies I've heard about heaven, I was intrigued to learn that all creation worships and gives glory to His majesty: trees sing, animals worship—what a great discovery! The Bible also says, "For the earnest expectation of creation is waiting for the manifestation of the sons of God." (Romans 8:19) It is said that when one gets to the other side, they hear and see the nature of God worshiping and adoring Him. If animals and plants praise Him, who are we not to hail His holy name? He is the monarch of Zion, the King of all glory, He that dwells in the midst of the cherubim.

Is heaven a real place?

Heaven is a literal place. It is not an illusion, as some think, but an inhabitation where God dwells. It is a place with its own characteristics, different from the earth. God created the earth beautiful and perfect, but things changed after He put a curse on the ground of the earth. The Bible says, "In the beginning God created the heavens and the earth." What a great discovery; there is more than one heaven. There is no specific location for these places called heavens, but I believe these heavens are spiritual habitations. Paul spoke of three heavens: "I know a man in Christ who fourteen years ago was caught up to the third heaven. Whether it was in the body or outside the body I don't know. God knows. He was caught up to paradise and heard unexpressible things; things no one is permitted to tell." (2 Corinthians 12:2-4) Could it be that Paradise is in the third heaven? Could it be that God is in the third heaven? Could it be that when Jesus went to prepare a place for us, He included Paradise in the design? Well, I guess we will find out when we get to heaven.

The kingdom of Christ

Imagine a kingdom ruled and governed by Christ. A kingdom where there is no sickness, no sorrow, and no pain whatsoever; how my soul longs for such a place. Many people will tell you how tired they are of this planet Earth, how they long for Jesus to come back and establish His kingdom that shall never end. When the time is right, Jesus is going to come back and execute His judgment on all things, and that will be the beginning of an everlasting kingdom.

Territorial Warfare

"For we wrestle not against flesh and blood, but against principalities, against powers, against the rulers of the darkness of this world, against spiritual wickedness in high places." (Ephesians 6:12)

What comes to your mind when you think about warfare? Have you ever imagined warfare in the context of territory? The word "territory" means a geographic area that a person or organization is responsible for in the course of work. It means someone is in control. Do you think God is in control on the earth? Territorial warfare is a very complex subject to speak about or engage in. Believers do not cover or engage in this type of warfare. Are we ignorant or afraid of territorial spirits? Do we understand what we should do to engage in this warfare? When looking at scripture for insight, there is not much other than a few important passages that discuss and affirm the reality associated with this type of warfare. Scripture affirms there are territorial spirits. Territorial spirits are described as demonic spirits said to control certain activities in the territory. They have the ability to manipulate what happens in the territory, the outcomes of people's lives, and circumstances at large. If we want revival in our world, then we should engage in this type of warfare however, this warfare requires a lot of spiritual understanding so that we don't fight ignorantly. All past stories of the move of God were a result of people who engaged in territorial warfare. It is important for us to know that every territory will always bow to the greater priesthood (whether good or bad).

Judgments of God

What comes to your mind when you think about judgment? How does one live with the knowledge that we will be judged by God at the end of time? How do we please God to make sure we secure His good judgment? Do you imagine God sitting on His throne and pronouncing judgments on His creation? Judgment for me is what brings balance to the imbalance caused by right and wrong. What is judgment for you? Do you see judgment as something right to do to correct wrong?

In human society, we perceive God not to be a God who can judge or cast one into hellfire. All the theories about hell are mere speculations in modern minds or throughout all generations of men. We understand there is life after death, but we don't perceive that we can be cast into hellfire as a judgment for our sins. Do you see hell and heaven as good judgments from God? If we believe there is a God in heaven, then we ought to think of this God as a person with principles and a way in which He disciplines wrong. I have come to believe that when one disciplines, for example, their children, it could be explained as good judgment.

One of the greatest truths about God is that He is Love. God reveals His love to us in different ways. We cannot imagine God to be a God who destroys or brings terrible judgment. To be honest, most of us know the love side of God, not the judgment side. This is good, but we must not forget that God is a judge, and as a judge, He has to do some things according to justice. For example, when men sinned and God wanted to judge them, there was imbalance in the justice system of heaven for this reason:

- Judgment says, "The wages of sin is death." (Romans 6:23)
- Mercy says, "Mercy prevails over judgment." (James 2:13)
- Love would say, "Men cannot die because You love them."

Now, to balance these three, God decided to leave His glory in heaven, put on flesh, and die for men whom He had created. In dying, the claims of divine justice were balanced.

---

1. Dr Myles Munroe, "Understanding the purpose of Man" (New Kensington, PA, USA: Whitaker House,

2001). www.whitakerhouse.com

1. Lifehopeandtruth.com/the last enemy

Thank you for reading this book!

Don't miss out!

Visit the website below and you can sign up to receive emails whenever Tumisang Mabe publishes a new book. There's no charge and no obligation.

https://books2read.com/r/B-A-GRUZ-BTKMF

BOOKS 2 READ

Connecting independent readers to independent writers.

www.ingramcontent.com/pod-product-compliance
Lightning Source LLC
LaVergne TN
LVHW010459160826
845677LV00012B/2553

* 9 7 9 8 2 3 0 7 9 7 6 2 3 *